Chickens

Julie Murray

Abdo
FARM ANIMALS
Kids

abdopublishing.com

Published by Abdo Kids, a division of ABDO, PO Box 398166, Minneapolis, Minnesota 55439.
Copyright © 2016 by Abdo Consulting Group, Inc. International copyrights reserved in all countries.
No part of this book may be reproduced in any form without written permission from the publisher.

Printed in the United States of America, North Mankato, Minnesota.

052015

092015

THIS BOOK CONTAINS
RECYCLED MATERIALS

Photo Credits: iStock, Science Source, Shutterstock

Production Contributors: Teddy Borth, Jennie Forsberg, Grace Hansen

Design Contributors: Candice Keimig, Dorothy Toth

Library of Congress Control Number: 2014960330

Cataloging-in-Publication Data

Murray, Julie.

 Chickens / Julie Murray.

  p. cm. -- (Farm animals)

ISBN 978-1-62970-938-3

Includes index.

1. Chickens--Juvenile literature.   I. Title.

636.5--dc23

                    2014960330

Table of Contents

Chickens 4

A Chicken's Life. 22

Glossary. 23

Index 24

Abdo Kids Code. 24

Chickens

Chickens live on a farm.

Some chickens are brown or white. Others are black. Some have many colors.

Chickens have a **comb** on their heads. They also have a **wattle**. Both are red.

Girl chickens are called hens. Boys are roosters. Babies are chicks.

hen

rooster

chicks

11

Roosters say,

"cock-a-doodle-doo."

Hens say, "cluck."

Chickens stay in a **coop**.

This keeps them safe.

They eat **grains** and grass.

They eat bugs too!

Hens lay eggs.

Kyle eats eggs for breakfast!

19

Have you seen chickens

on a farm?

A Chicken's Life

drink water

lay eggs

eat grain

wake everyone up

Glossary

comb
a soft part on top of the head of some birds.

grain
the seeds of plants that are used for food.

coop
a small building where chickens are kept.

wattle
skin that hangs from the head or neck of some birds.

Index

chick 10

color 6

coop 14

farm 4, 20

food 16

head 8

hen 10

noise 12

products 18

rooster 10

abdokids.com

Use this code to log on to abdokids.com and access crafts, games, videos, and more!

Abdo Kids Code:
FHK9383